MONKEY VS. ROBOT

JAMES KOCHALKA

TOP SHELF PRODUCTIONS
MARIETTA, GA

MONKEY VS. ROBOT

PUBLISHED BY

TOP SHELF PRODUCTIONS
P.O. BOX 1282
MARIETTA, GA
30061-1282

www.topshelfcomix.com

EDITED BY CHRIS STAROS
PRODUCTION DESIGN BY BRETT WARNOCK,
CRAIG THOMPSON AND JAMES KOCHALKA

KOCHALKA, JAMES
MONKEY VS. ROBOT/ JAMES KOCHALKA
ISBN: 1-891830-15-5
GRAPHIC NOVELS, CARTOONS

SECOND PRINTING, PRINTED IN CANADA

FOR
3FD91

"Why can't we all love each other,
Monkey and our Robot brother?"

boom

boom
boom
boom

boom

KLACK

thump

boom

boom boom
klackity klack

boom boom
thump thump

boom boom boom
klackity klack
thump

boom boom boom boom

chucka
chucka
chucka

chucka
chuka
chuka
KLOONG
shzip
whiRR

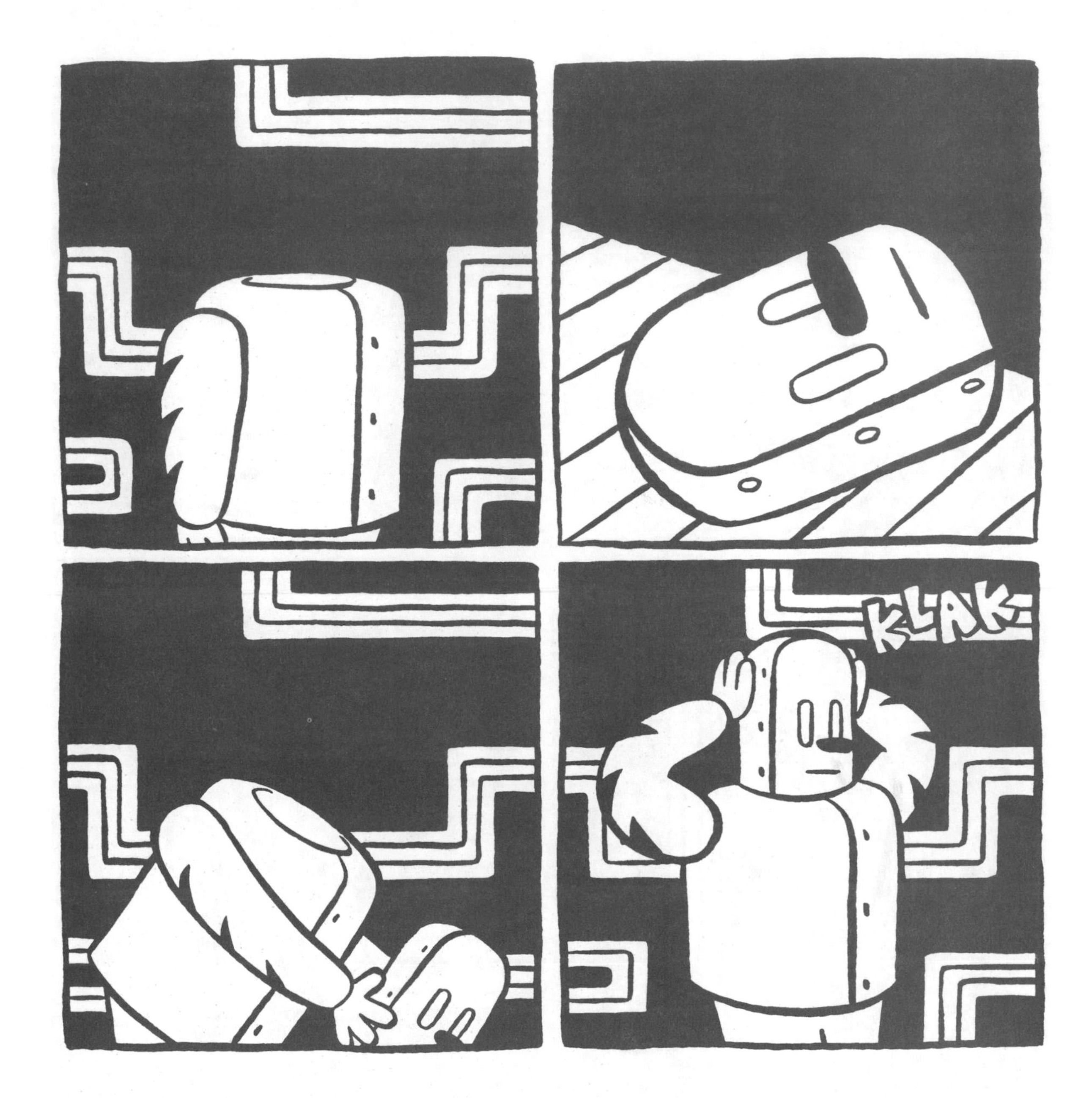
KLAK

THE FUTURE IS NOW!

CLANK
CLANK

CLANK

CLANK
CLANK

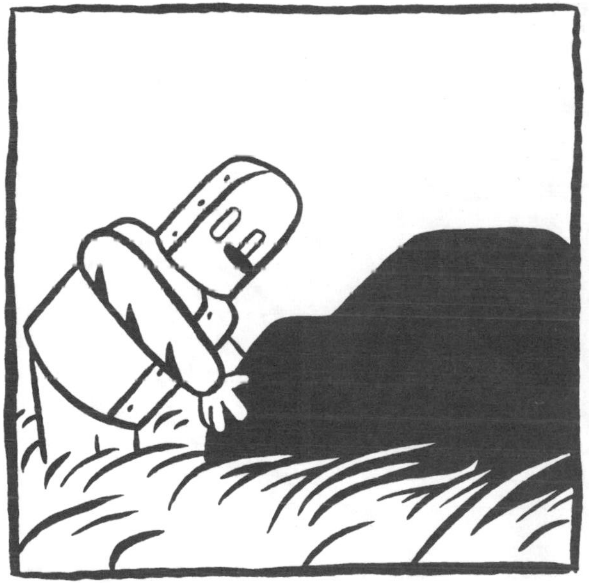

BLURP

GAZHUNK
GAZHUNK

KLOONG
KLOONG
chug
chug
chug

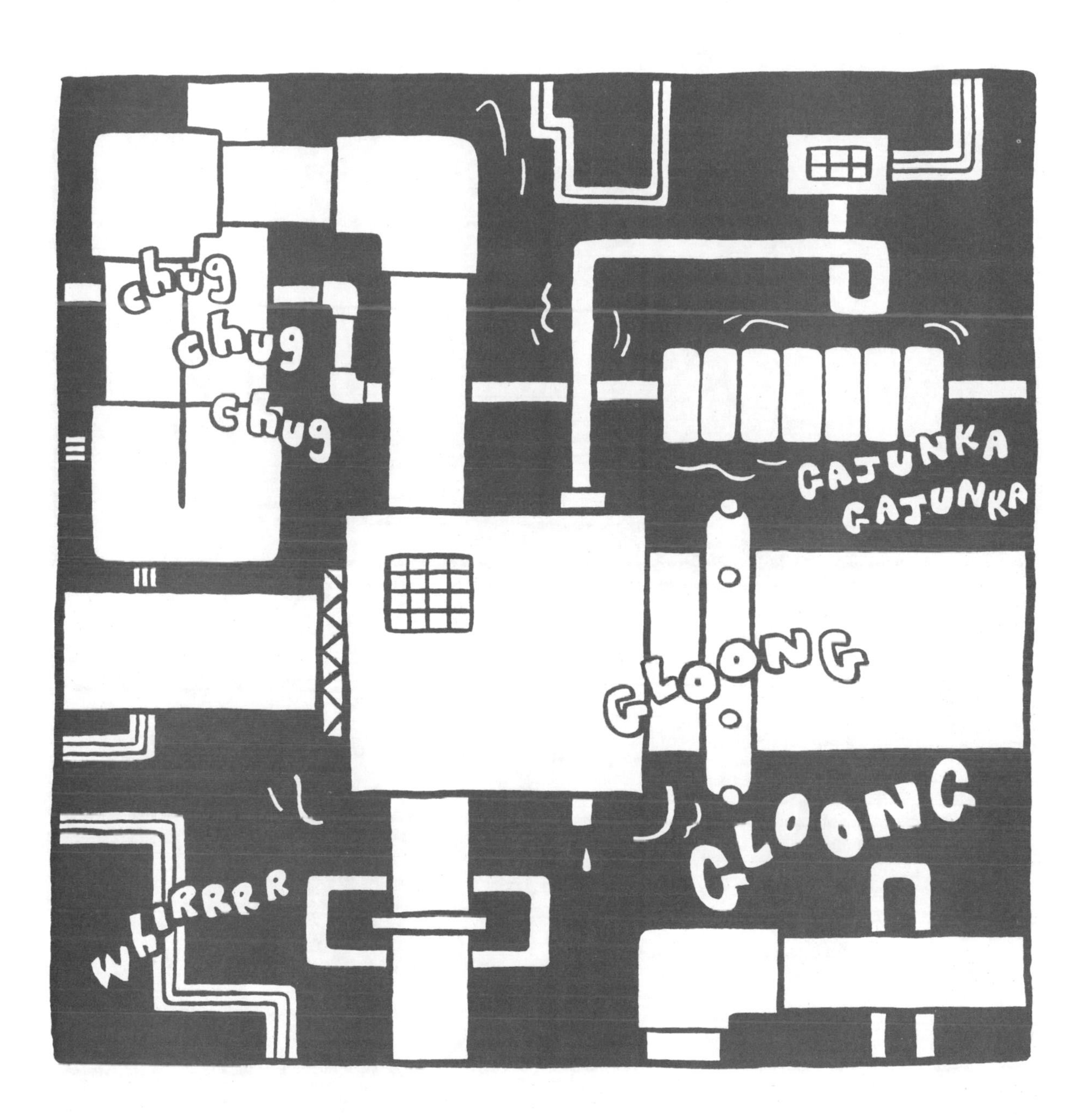
chug
chug
chug
GAJUNKA
GAJUNKA
GLOONG
GLOONG
WHIRRRR

RUMBLE

bLORP

bLORP

BLORP
BLORP
GLORP

hop

shake
shake

blORP

Rustle
Rustle

Peek!

?
Snif
Snif

chip chip chee

cheeeeeee...

SKRONK

SKRONK
SKRONK

SKRONK

SKRONK

chip chip SKRONK!
?
!

GRRRRRRR

SLIP

CRUNCH

BZZT
ZRP

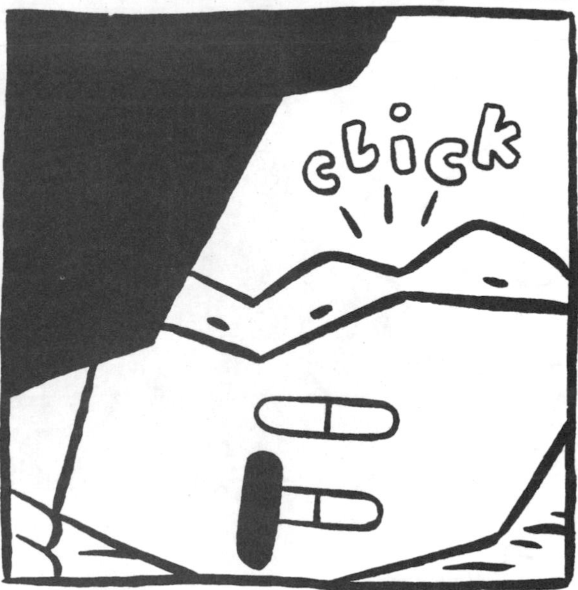
click

beep
beep
bip

RECEIVING TRANSMISSION

ROBOT DOWN

INITIATING INVESTIGATION

SKID!
THUMP

MONKEY EXCREMENT

CLICK
WHIRRR

BEGIN EXTERMINATION

HUP TWO THREE FOUR
BONK
thump

A COCONUT?

CLONK

FUMP

RUN

SWOO
SWOOSH
WOOSH
SWOOSH

WUMP

KLANG

KLANG
KLANG
KLANG

WUMP

KLANG
KLANG
KLANG

CLANK

SCRAPE
gRNt

PUSH

KLANK

GRRRRRRRRRRRR

NO

GRRRR

EEEEEE

CRACKLE

NO

ARR

ZING
CLUNK

NZERF

YRRZT

!

Chee chee!

ATTACK!

KLANK

CRUNCH

KICK
POW

SKLUTCH

CLANK
CLANK
CLANK

CLONK

BONK

DOOMF

WUMP
GRR

GRRR

KRAK
ZZRK

ZZORP
FZZT

CRACKLE

WUMP

TRIP

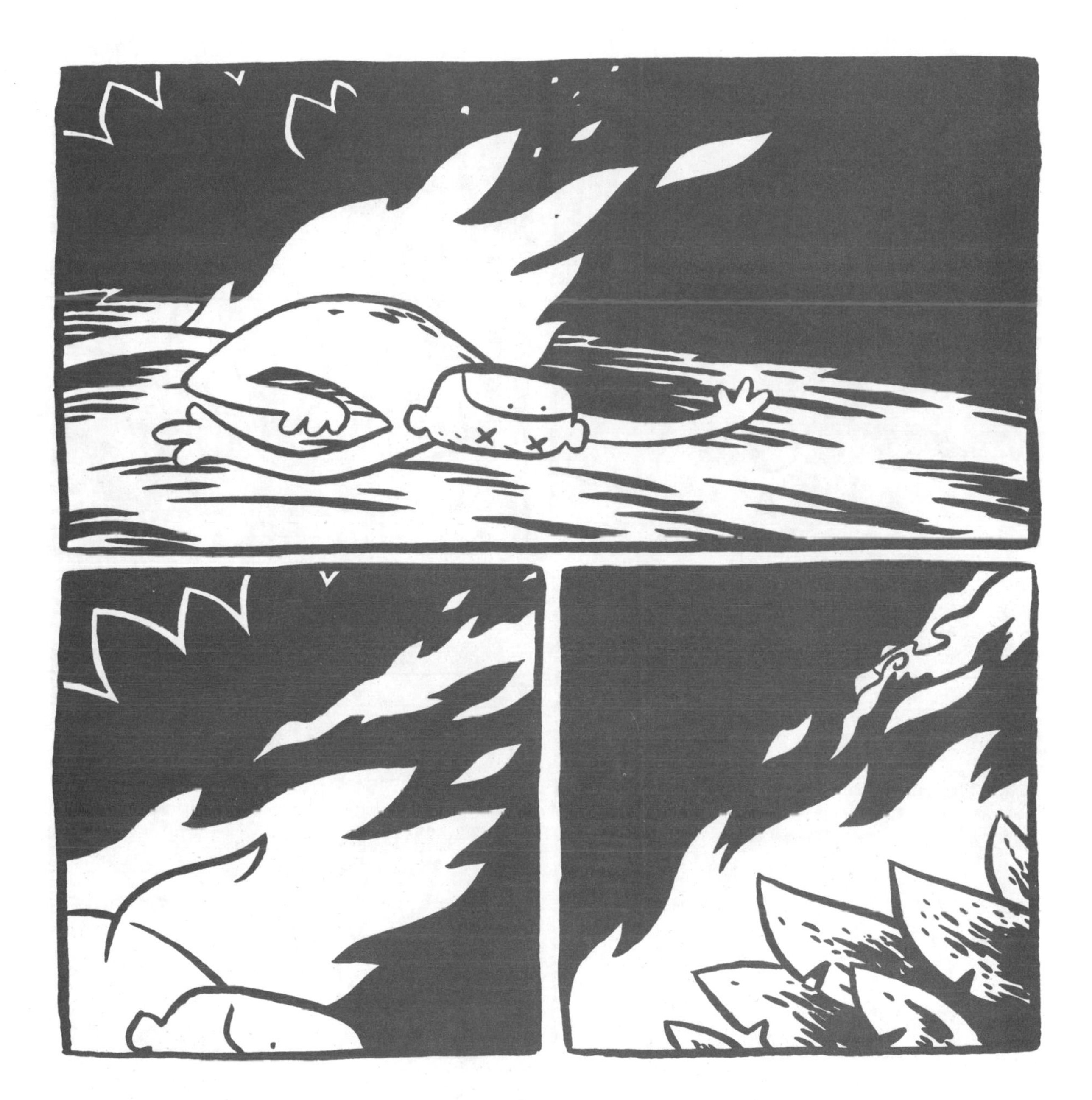

LET NO MONKEY ESCAPE!

ENTER THE FIRE!

Gasp. .
huf

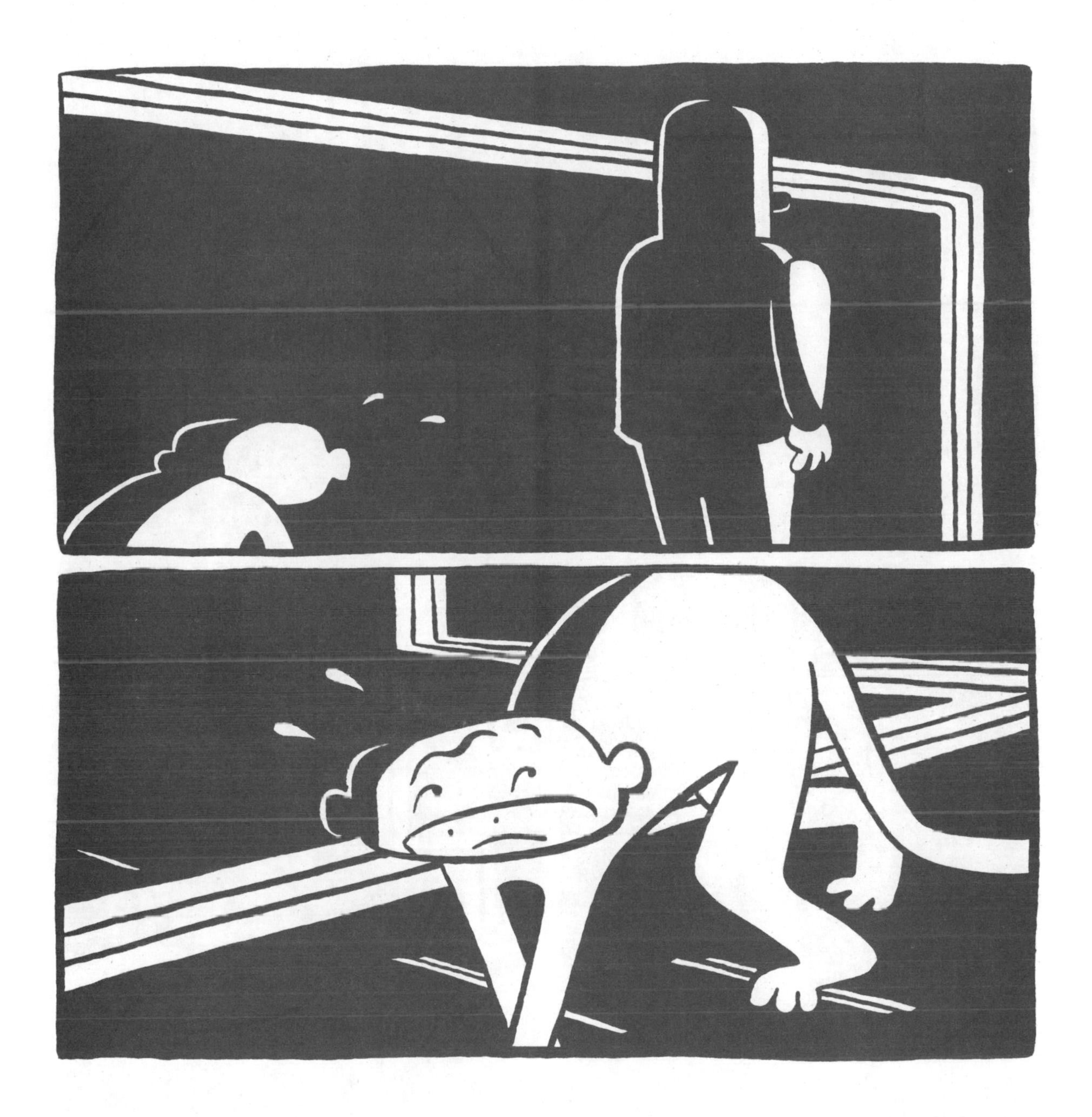

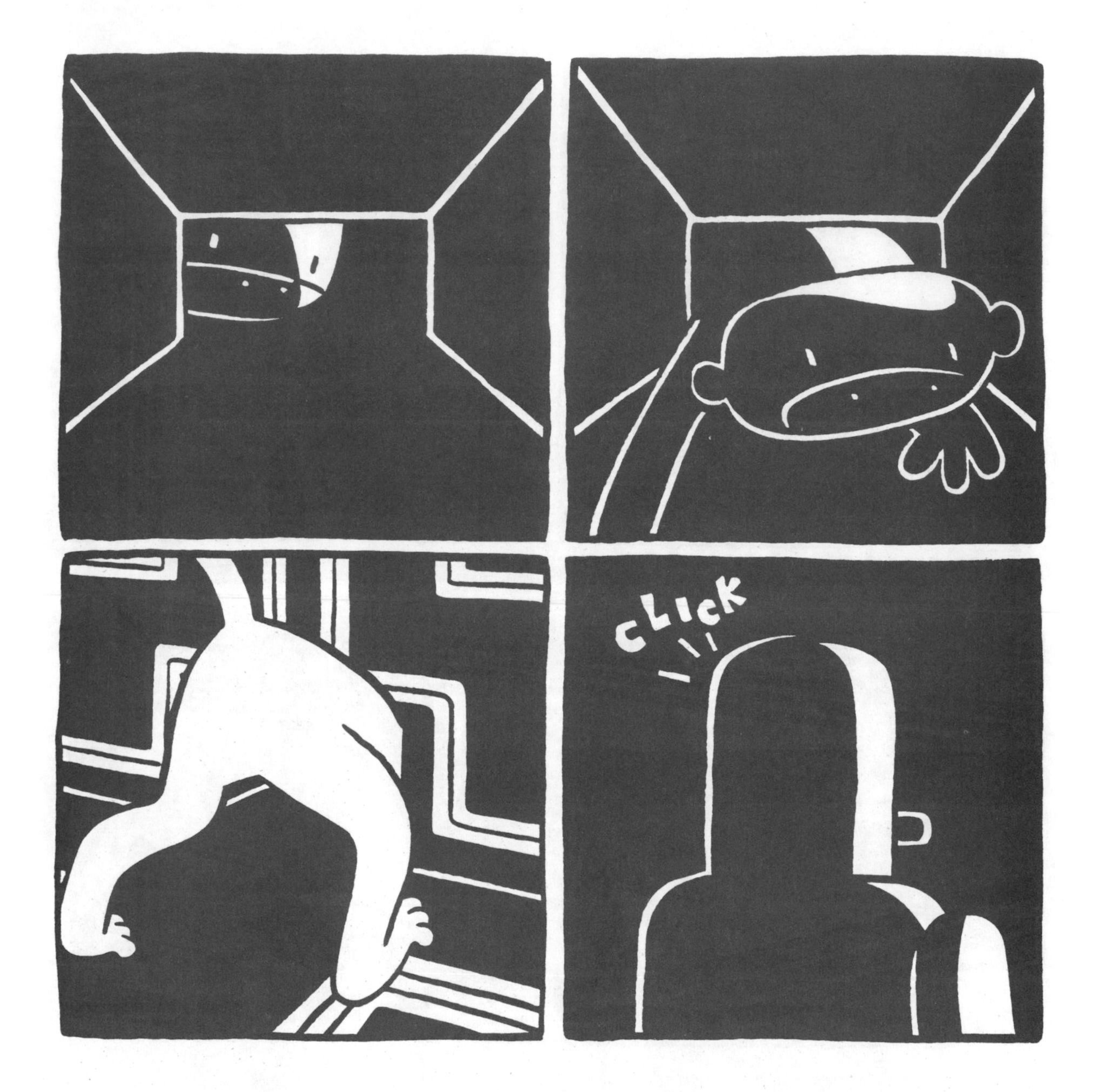
CLICK

Z Z P

SIMIAN

I AM THE MOTHER

YOU ARE THE DIRT

YOU ARE THE PAST

NOTHING

DIRTY FLESH WILL SURRENDER TO METAL FUTURITY

CRYSTALLINE PERFECTION

SIMIAN EXTINCTION

eek!

CRUSHING

CRUSH

Yipe!

LUNGE

HEY

STOP TOUCHING ME!

GET OFF

OFF

STOP
NO
KRAK

KLONK
IMBECILE-
ROAR

BOOM

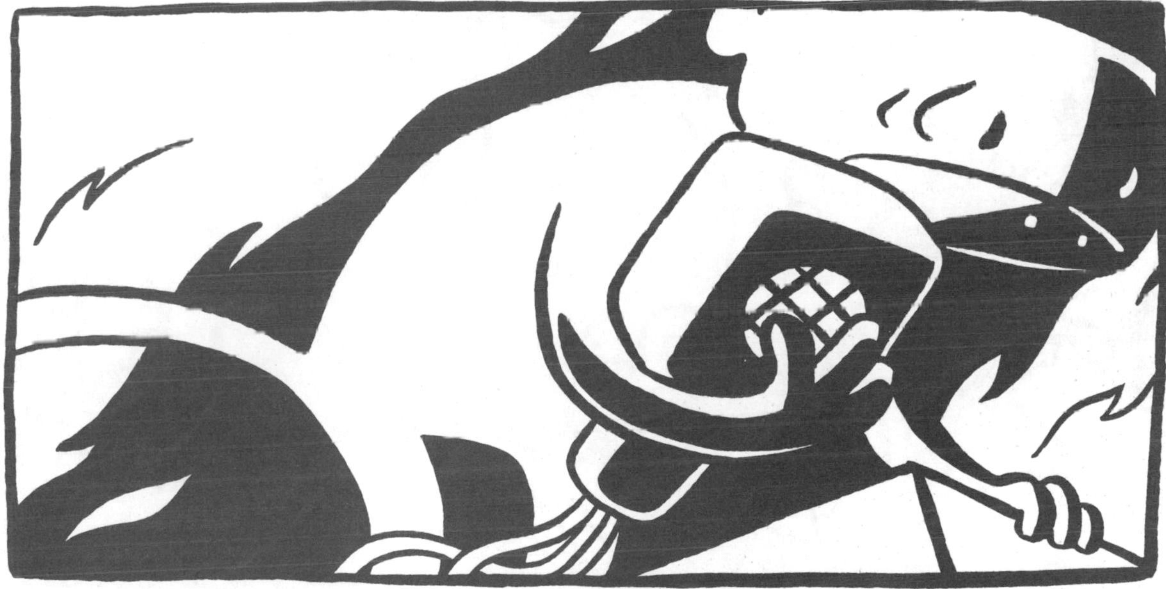

BOOM

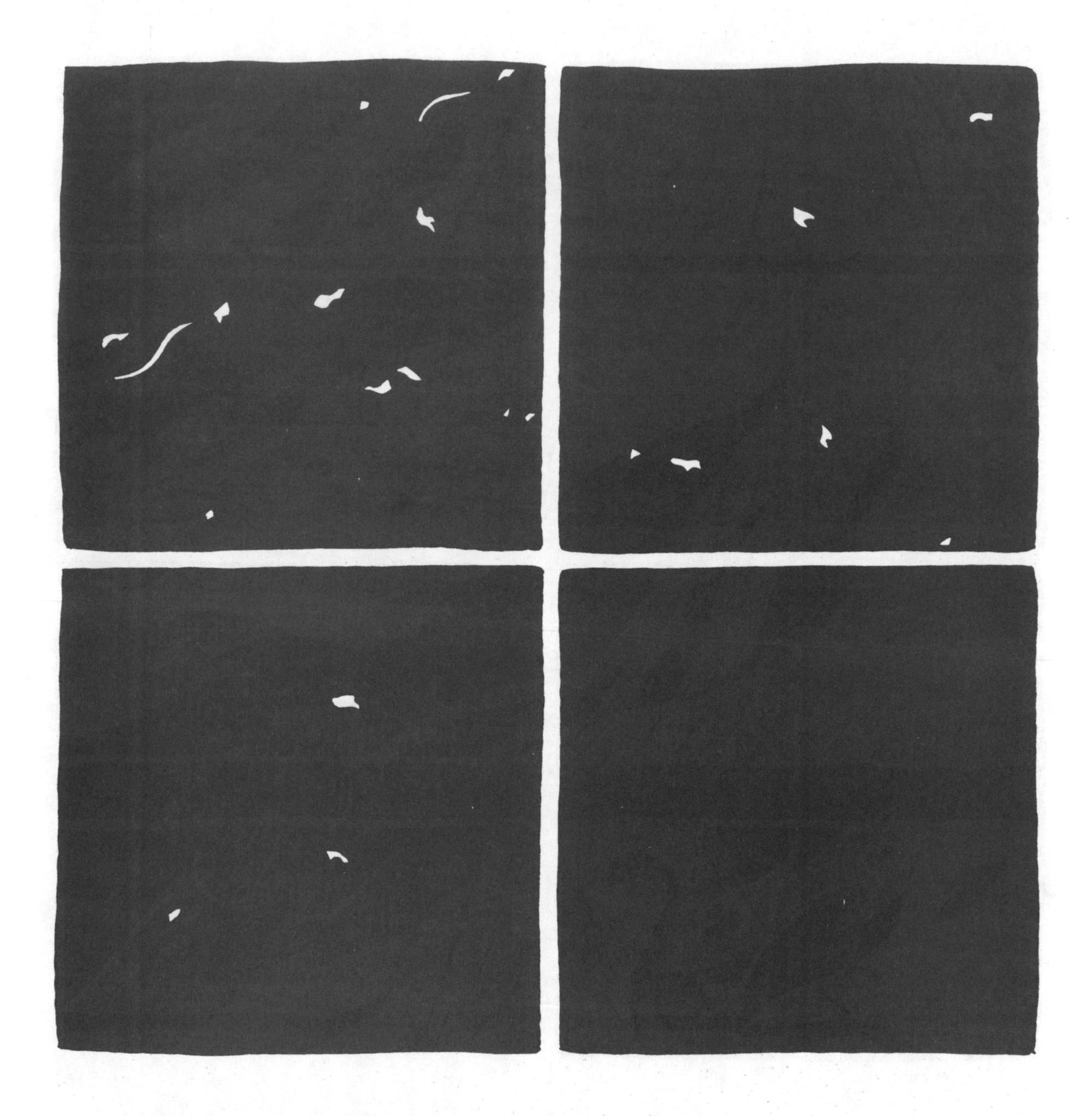

EPILOGUE:

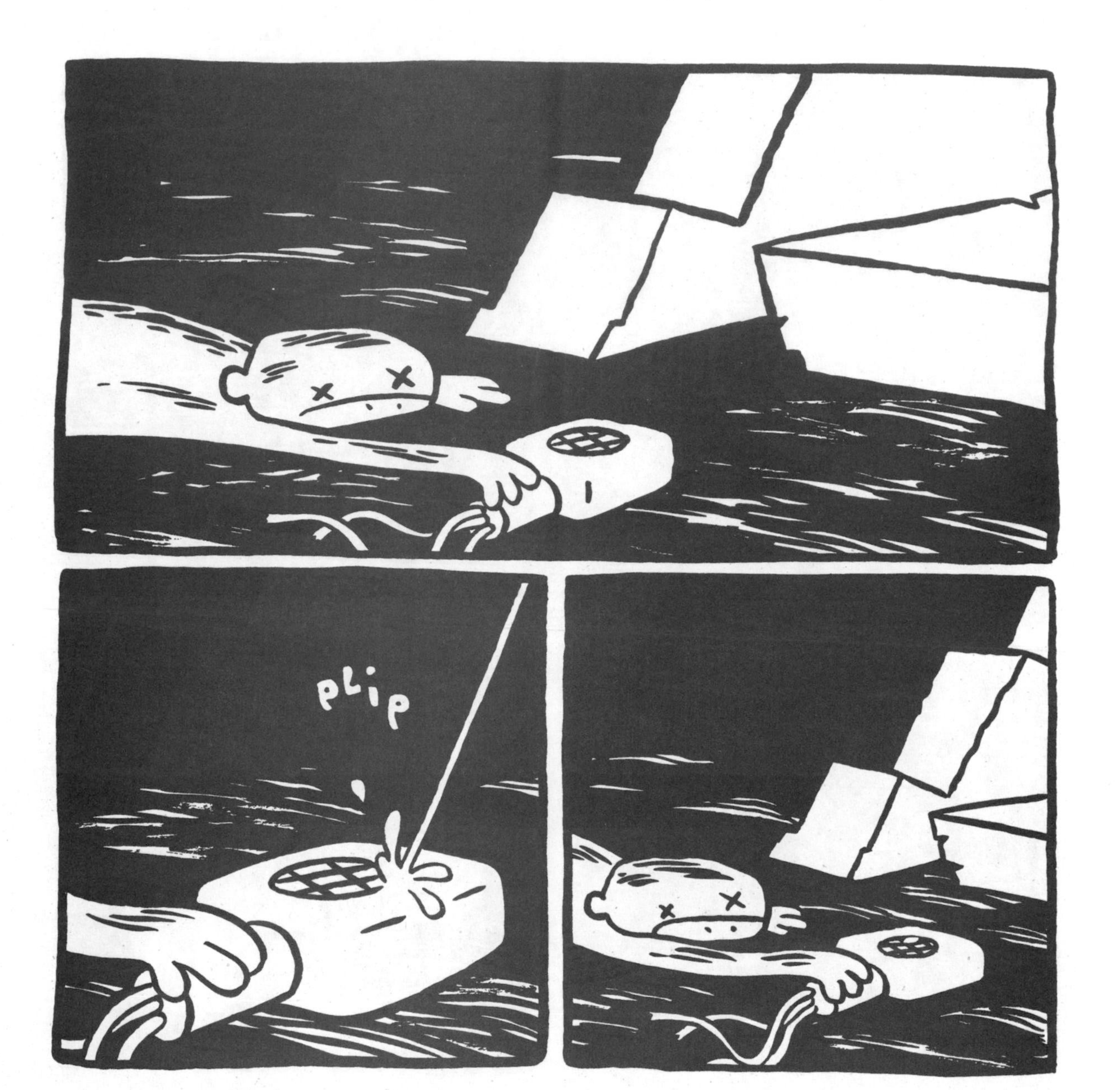
plip

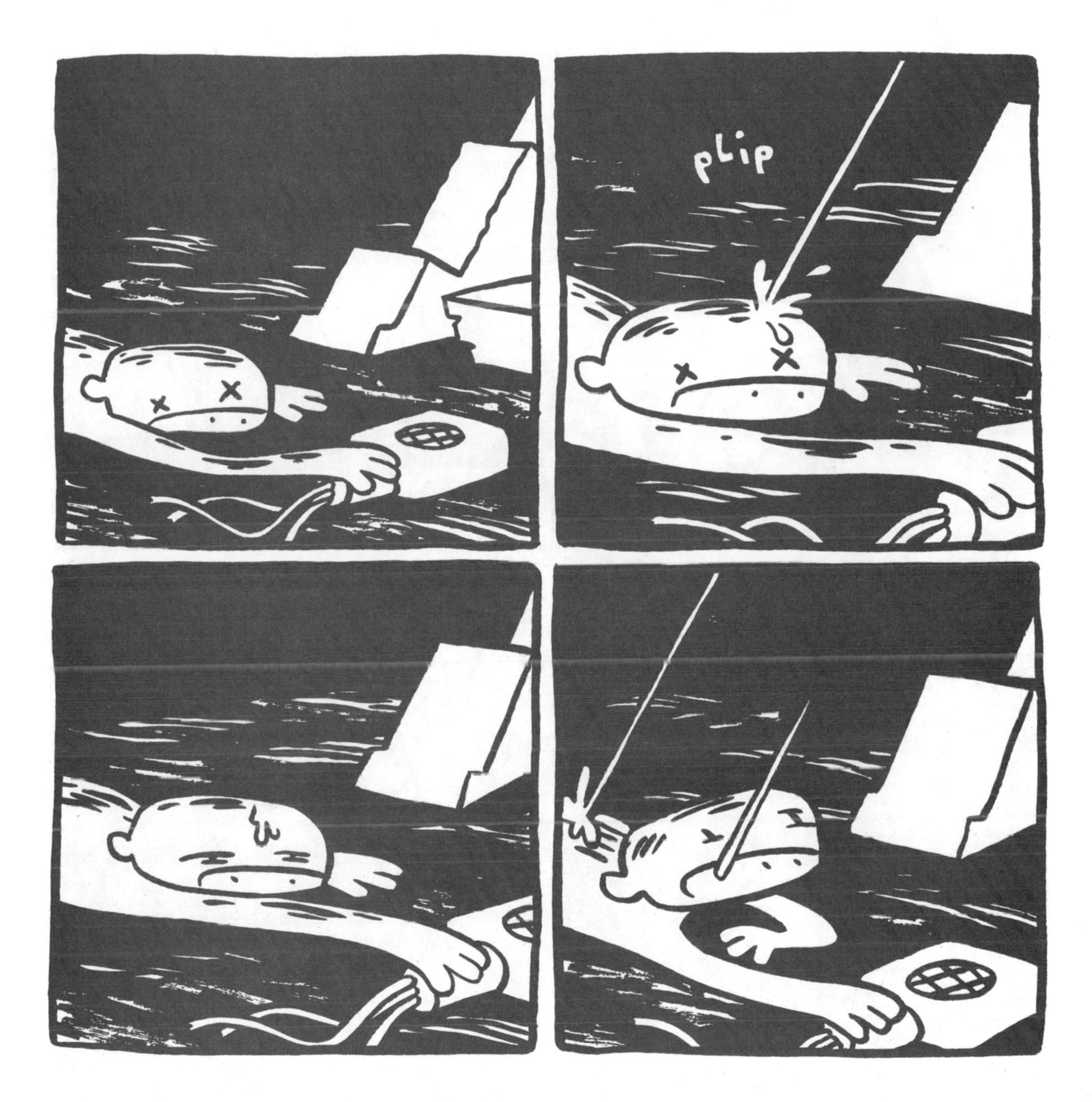
plip

PLIP
PLIP
PLIP
PLIP

whee
ek
ek!

THANK YOU: AMY KING, SPANDY, JASON X-12, PISTOL, BRIAN RALPH & CAVE-IN, NATE POMMER, PETER AND TARQUIN KATIS, GEOFFREY MARSLETT, MARK MAREK, PASCAL, CRESTON & KERRIE MATHES, DIET COKE, NON, SOUTH UNION STREET, ERIC B. RADFORD, TOM DEVLIN, MICHEL VRANA, JEFF MASON (THE PUBLISHER WHO CARES?!), CHRIS DUFFY, YEBO, CASEY SILER & THE BURLINGTON FREE PRESS, PRACTICE TRACK, REVOLUTION, INK 19, VICE, V-MAG, NEW GUY, CAMPFIRES, NYC, TRIAGE, 6H PENCILS, ULTRA BIDÉ, ANDY KONKY KRU, CHARLES BERBERIAN, MELTDOWN, BIG PLANET COMICS, THE MILLION YEAR PICNIC, PANIC ATTACKS, SWEET LOVE, WINSOR & NEWTON, JOSÉ RUI FERNANDES, JANUS, FILIPA THE MECHANICAL MONKEY, LOS ANGELES, MILLENNIUM BUDWEISER, SUNSHINE, CASIOS, PORTUGAL, CHRIS OARR & THE COMIC BOOK LEGAL DEFENSE FUND, DARKNESS, FUN, ATARI 2600, THE ZAMBONIS, CARA BRUCE, RYKODISC & DREAMWORKS, SLEEP, MEGAN WEBER & DAVE ROMAN, QUAKE2, KINKO'S, BAG OF PANTIES, LANCE RICHBOURG, CROW BOOKSHOP, JAWRSH, YOLANDA & CHERRY TART, ABE LINCOLN, MISSY BLY, BUELL ST, LAKE CHAMPLAIN, mp3.com/jks, BEAUTY, NIGHTMARES, WORRYING, CONFUSION, MY WONDERFUL PARENTS, COLIN CLARY, LI'L SCOTTY, PETER & JANE & JOHNNY, LOUIS RIEL, THE INK TANK, GLUE STICKS, MY FANS AND EVERYONE AND EVERYTHING THAT HAD ANY EFFECT ON ME, HOWEVER SLIGHT, IN THE YEAR IT TOOK ME TO COMPLETE THIS BOOK...

JAMES KOCHALKA GREW UP IN SPRINGFIELD, THE EIGHTH LARGEST TOWN IN VERMONT. HIS MOTHER SAYS HE BEGAN DRAWING BEFORE HE LEARNED HOW TO WALK. BY THE AGE OF NINE, HE HAD DRAWN HIS FIRST FULL LENGTH GRAPHIC NOVEL. ONCE, HE WAS PUNCHED IN THE NOSE. HE NOW RESIDES IN BURLINGTON, VERMONT WITH HIS WIFE AMY AND THEIR CAT SPANDY. AFTER WORKING AS A WAITER IN A CHINESE RESTAURANT FOR SIX YEARS, HE QUIT AND BEGAN WORKING ON THIS BOOK.